WORLD GUITAR

GUITARIST'S GUIDE TO THE TRADITIONAL STYLES OF CULTURES AROUND THE WORLD

BY GREG P. HERRIGES

T0040791

ISBN-13: 978-0-634-07385-4
ISBN-10: 0-634-07385-4

HAL•LEONARD® CORPORATION

7777 W. BLUEMOUND RD. P.O. BOX 13819 MILWAUKEE, WI 53213

In Australia Contact:
Hal Leonard Australia Pty. Ltd.
4 Lentara Court
Cheltenham, Victoria, 3192 Australia
Email: ausadmin@halleonard.com

Visit Hal Leonard Online at
www.halleonard.com

ACKNOWLEDGMENTS

Thanks to everyone who made this project possible, including but not limited to:

Indian Music Society of Minnesota (IMSOM)

Shirley Massie, for the photos and magic guitar

All other donors of images and knowledge (listed within)

All the talented, patient, and open-eared folks at Hal Leonard Corporation

CONTENTS

INTRODUCTION

The world has always been shrinking. The exchange of arts and ideas between cultures started long before the age of exploration and intercontinental travel, and the trend is racing toward some kind of culmination in the twenty-first century. In today's age of communication, borders hardly exist; hardly any culture in the world is inaccessible. That can be great news for musicians.

Of course, there are downsides to globalization and cross-cultural contact—especially when it leads to one culture devouring another. But hopefully, previously unknown forms of expression are constantly being discovered and exposed to those who wouldn't have known them in an isolated society. We should accept and respect that new knowledge. For the forward-looking musician, new ways of playing and seeing are priceless. The universal language of music reaches beyond borders and languages to express the inexpressible. Music is cultural, but it transcends culture!

Traditional music should never be lost, but influence can't be stopped. Without an infusion of African-American blues and rock 'n' roll, Afropop would not be quite the same. The rich Hindustani traditions of North India would not be what they are without a Persian influence. (Neither would the Western orchestra, for that matter!) Music always reflects the soul of the people and the place from which it comes, and any cultural melting pot will produce a fusion of sounds, just as America has. Fusions of old and new are constantly developing, too; the mixing of modern electronic grooves with traditional sounds from around the world is one example. While the world shrinks, musical horizons should expand.

This book/CD is meant to show you some ways that you can start expanding your horizons as a guitarist. Use it to learn new techniques and enhance your creative skills on the instrument, or let it begin a journey of deeper discovery that will lead to a truer understanding of the stringed (and other) traditions of the world. Of course, one book will never cover the entire world of music, and some of the great guitar traditions must be neglected for another volume. I have covered plenty of existing guitar traditions, but the biggest challenge, and great fulfillment, has come from adapting the guitar to the music of other, non-guitar styles.

The book is arranged by region, not necessarily by difficulty or familiarity, so feel free to jump around it if that suits you. There will be certain concepts that reappear, aspects that many different musical examples have in common. Some of these are fundamental and structural, like the prevalent 6/8 feel in many styles, or the fact that much of the world's music outside the West has a modal, rather than harmonic, orientation, with a drone (instead of moving chords) supporting the melody. Others are recurring technical directions, like the playing of open strings between melody notes, or a certain picking technique that emulates another instrument. All of this will be explained in detail as it comes up.

Most of the traditions we're touching on are aural, not written, and can only be truly mastered by immersion, with the support of a teacher or a musical community. This taste of world music will give you a starting point. If you like what falls under your fingers, dig deeper! Consult the "Recommended Media" section for more examples of each style. Remember that this book is like an international buffet, just a sample of the endless variety and depth of musical "soul food" that is out there for the aspiring connoisseur. It can't be devoured all at once without losing its essence. But enough talk—it's time to make music!

HOW TO USE THIS BOOK/CD

The music in this book is taught mostly in Western terms of melody, harmony, and rhythm. It is geared toward intermediate and advanced guitar players of all styles, but other musicians and the astute layperson will benefit from it as well. The guitarist who will get the most out of it will already:

- read standard music notation and/or tab;

- have a basic knowledge of chords, scales, and intervals;

- be comfortable with chord strumming, single-note picking, and some fingerstyle playing;

- have an open mind and an appetite for new ways of making music.

In our Western musical terms, we can say that each new piece of music will have some clearly describable aspects, to be listed at the start of each transcription:

- a guitar **tuning**, standard or otherwise;

- a **scale** or **key** associated with the piece of music;

- a style of **picking** execution (with a plectrum, fingerstyle, or hybrid);

- a characteristic **sound** that (ideally) calls for a certain type of guitar or effect setting (acoustic steel-string, electric with clean tone, etc.). As much as possible we'll stick to acoustic.

You'll get the blanks filled in on these and many more details as you progress, and some very relevant background on each style and its origins will be provided. First, listen to the full demo on the CD to get the feel of the music. After each transcription is a written breakdown of its essential parts, and tips on how to play the piece effectively. The CD also has slow demos of the most challenging bits of each piece. Scales and short technique demos are recorded wherever they're relevant. It's best to try playing along with the track only after you've digested all this info. Wherever there are backing tracks or multiple guitars, they are panned on separate sides of the mix, so you can isolate one or play the main part along with the others.

CD CREDITS

Greg Herriges:	guitars, flutes, and some percussion support
John Wright:	bass, guitar on tracks 29–30 (Celtic)
A. Pavan:	tabla
Troy Berg:	drum kit, dumbek, and all things shaken and jingled

Recorded at the Dining Room/New Folk Studios, Minneapolis, MN
Engineered and mastered by John Wright

 Standard tuning: (low to high) E–A–D–G–B–E

Track 1

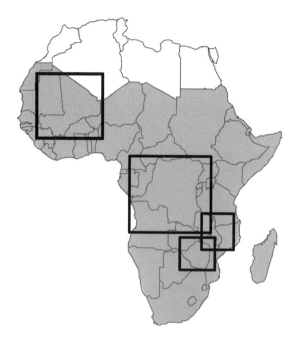

When scholars talk about the cradles of musical civilization, two non-Western areas most often come up: the Middle East and Africa. Africa, musically speaking, can be considered the area of the continent south of Egypt, Libya, Algeria, and Morocco (countries whose music has a strong Middle Eastern influence). Musical traditions from the vast sub-Saharan region have enough in common that we can group a few of them together on these pages, but as you'll see, there's an amazing diversity of African guitar music, now undergoing an explosion of variety and popularity. It tends to have a relaxed but upbeat lilting quality that typifies African music in general—not to mention complex rhythms and mind-blowing techniques.

Six-string guitars were first brought to West Africa by Portuguese sailors in the 1700s, but the stringed and other traditions of African music are far more ancient. Many styles of African guitar music mix those ancient traditions with modern influences from all over the world, but each still holds on to its own regional flavor. Ironically, so much of the music of the Americas—blues, jazz, rock 'n' roll, and many genres of Latin music— grew from African origins, and has now come full circle to influence many African guitarists, who infused it with a fresh spirit. The results are amazing.

WEST AFRICAN ACOUSTIC WONDERS

This first introduction to African guitar will involve some interesting techniques. As the guitar was introduced into music of the Manding people of the continent's northwestern coast, it took on the flavors of the indigenous instruments that preceded it, including the *balafon* (a wooden xylophone) and the *kora*, a kind of harp/lute with twenty-one strings arranged on two sides of a long neck. The music traditionally played on these instruments accompanied ceremonial singing with hypnotic grooves, intertwining melodies, and polyrhythms.

Kora

The kora technique is especially effective on guitar. It often involves a kind of quick, percussive grace note that is plucked and sustained into the next note, then muted immediately for a dissonant, almost buzzing effect. (Buzzing and rattling sounds are prevalent and preferred in traditional African music.) Picking is done with the thumb and index finger, as in much Afro-acoustic guitar. The following tune showcases a few different ways to approach the kora technique, in the style of some of the masters of guitar-rich Mali and a genre sometimes called Malian blues, mostly because it's based in the minor pentatonic scale (as is most American blues).

Tuning:	standard
Key/Scale:	A minor pentatonic (A–C–D–E–G)
Picking:	fingerstyle (thumb and forefinger)
Sound:	acoustic steel-string guitar

MALI SONG

Moderately ♩ = 123

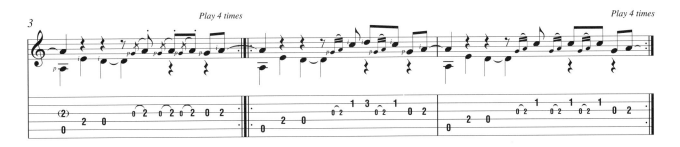

"Mali Song" Performance Notes

This repeating vamp is played with four increasingly involved versions of the kora technique. The first is with hammer-ons that, as much as possible, should be stopped as soon as the hammered note is hit. Do this with a combination of left- and right-hand muting: release pressure with the fretting finger immediately after you perform the hammer-on on the G string, but also let your picking thumb and/or index finger rest on that string between plucks. (Suggested picking fingers are shown next to the notes on the staff: *p* = thumb; *i* = index finger.)

The next variation (meas. 4) expands on the first and adds a note. The hammer-on gets muted and the C note comes quickly after it, followed by a D on fret 3. Every instance of what was a hammer-on in the first variation becomes a flurry of three notes. Play them in fast succession without letting them blur together as a chord. This requires your right (picking) hand to dig in and pluck a little harder—but not aggressively—to get the percussive quality across.

Variation 3 (meas. 6) uses the kind of kora technique you'll hear most often from West African guitarists. The left (fretting) hand shifts positions, so you can pull the grace note and the target note on adjacent strings for a clean, percussive "fling." (Left-hand fingerings are shown above the staff.) Pick your pinky finger off the D string right away, so the G note doesn't ring out. You'll need that finger anyway, to jump to the C on the next string and back down again for the next "fling." All that finger jumping helps you play nice and staccato (short).

The fourth variation (meas. 8) simply adds more of the same technique on the lower notes.

Notice the position of the picking hand on the strings: the thumb and index finger sit right next to each other, so they can pick adjacent strings or alternate-pick notes on one string. The rest of the fingers rest on the sidelines. This style of picking is distinctly native African (even though this hand clearly isn't).

AFROPOP: CONGOLESE AND ZIMBABWEAN RUMBA

The electrified music we know as Afropop comes in different regional flavors from all over the continent. The most influential and characteristic brand of Afropop grew up in the Congo, where bands mixed Cuban dance music (which itself had been African-influenced) with already-developed local styles. The resulting music was first dubbed "African rumba" after one of the Cuban rhythms it assimilated. With more indigenous influence, it came to be known as *soukous*, among other things, and it was a sensation all over Africa in the 1970s and eighties. Its influence worldwide is still growing.

Kalimbas

Soukous music was adopted by east African countries like Uganda, Kenya, and Zimbabwe, where it took on a more energetic African groove and more of an interweaving between lead and rhythm guitarists and bass, slightly reminiscent of *mbira* playing. (The mbira or *kalimba*, an indigenous kind of thumb piano, is played in a style that usually involves two or three complementing melodies that play off each other rhythmically.)

The following example draws from Congolese and Zimbabwean rumba tunes. The chord progression is one of the upbeat African standards, I–IV–V–IV, repeating in variation as it would in the final section of a typical African rumba piece—the *seben*—when the beat picks up and the guitarists jam. Listen to the interplay between the two guitars and bass; they complement each other without imitation or competing for space, weaving around rather than bouncing off each other. The perfect musical relationship!

Tuning:	standard
Key:	E major
Picking:	flatpick
Sound:	Guitar 1 (rhythm): acoustic steel-string Guitar 2 (lead): electric with a clean tone and optional tight delay (one repetition)

SOUKOUS RUMBABWE

"Soukous Rumbabwe" Performance Notes

Play all these lines with a relaxed pick; keep your right hand loose and don't attack the strings. The rhythm guitar is basically moving between three barre chord positions, but changing the feel for each section. Most of the chord muting or stopping is done with the left hand, by lifting off the fretboard but not the strings, so you get *staccato* (short, choppy) effects as in the first upbeats in measure 1.

The same bouncy feel gets busier in section C, where the rhythm guitar throws in more choppy left-hand mutes, picking up the chord after almost every strum. Luckily this doesn't last too long, because it can be hard work for the thumb! Section D has the rhythm guitar *arpeggiating* (playing a chord one note at a time) and sliding in another typical pattern. These patterns change according to the lead guitar part.

Afropop lead guitar pointers: Keep left-hand trills and frills to a minimum (the notes and the rhythms do most of the talking); keep the groove happening while *syncopating* (accenting a weak beat or displacing the beat); and do not wiggle or bend the strings! Those of us who come from a rock or blues background may be tempted to add vibrato on every sustaining note. We must resist!

Lead patterns fall into repeated two- and four-measure groups that play as "question and answer" phrases. The first is a series of arpeggios that follow the main progression, with characteristic rests and offset beats. (Suggested picking patterns are shown under the staff.) Again, mutes are done with the fretting hand; the right hand floats around the neck pickup (where the neck ends on the body of the guitar—see photo). This typical picking position gives it that mellow Afropop tone.

Right-hand position near the neck pickup

When you start soloing in section C, you're playing more or less in a box of the E major pentatonic scale, but the chosen notes follow the changes of the chord progression. This holds true throughout the lead part as it moves up in section D to alternate between arpeggios and triplet figures.

A guitarist who wants to play lead in Afropop should get to know the guitar neck by heart: learn to play the basic major and minor chords in any position, for the sake of arpeggios; be able to play major scales in all positions and in *dyads* or *double stops* (two-note chords), especially *parallel 6ths* (a sequence of two-note groups made up of the first and sixth scale tones); and most importantly, know how to break up the groove into syncopated lines. Chord progressions are generally straight ahead, but the weaving of rhythms and melodies in African style is a fine and complex art.

SOLO ACOUSTIC "RUMBA"

Southeast Africa is rich in guitar traditions of all kinds, and solo acoustic fingerstyle playing is especially noteworthy. The Afropop movement in Central and East Africa was predated by a thriving acoustic guitar scene in the 1950s and sixties, after the instrument had been introduced by migrant workers in Congolese mining towns, and a growing economy made imported guitars accessible to local people. From there the guitar spread to the southeast, where musicians created a hybrid playing style all their own on inexpensive, sometimes homemade instruments. As in West Africa, traditional playing techniques were translated to the acoustic guitar in new and inventive ways.

The *mbira* (a.k.a. *kalimba* or *ikembe*) thumb piano, as described earlier, is played in such a way that alternate melodies complement and criss-cross each other. Solo guitarists from Southeastern Africa combined this kind of feel with the rumba-style rhythms that had already begun to seep into the African consciousness.

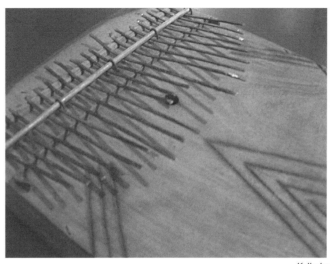

Kalimba

The next example introduces the capo, not to make your life difficult but because it's important in this music. Depending on the player, the capo usually sits between frets 5 and 8 to bring the guitar's pitch up and accommodate a vocal melody—but it's used in solo guitar music as well. (It also makes the guitar sound more like the higher-pitched thumb piano.)

This repeated pattern with subtle variations comes from the music of Malawi, in the style of players like Moya Aliya Malamusi and Daniel Kachamba.

Tuning:	standard
Key:	G major
Picking:	fingerstyle (thumb and forefinger)
Sound:	acoustic nylon-string

MALAWI SONG

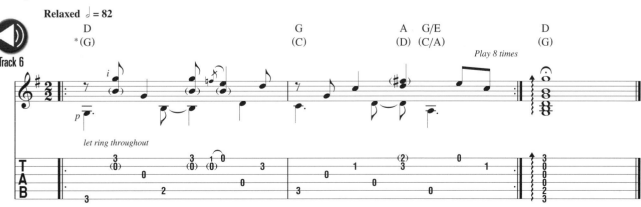

*Symbols in parentheses represent chord names respective to capoed guitar. Symbols above reflect actual sounding chords. Capoed fret is "0" in tab.

"Malawi Song" Performance Notes

Notice that the part isn't played exactly the same every time; in repeating forms like this there's room for a lot of subtle variation. It's played on a cheap nylon-string guitar with a thin neck (for many African guitarists this accommodates fretting with the thumb). The sonic character of such a guitar can be quite appropriate—in fact, just the right amount of buzzing frets and rattling hardware gives a sound more like the designed vibrations of the mbira and kora.

The capo is clamped on fret 7, and the left hand outlines G, C, and D chord positions (with a transitional C/A at the end of the pattern). The G chord position should be played with the third, second, and fourth fingers, leaving the index free to play that very cool pull-off from the dominant 7th to the 6th—something Americans might call bluesy, and in fact it shares some of the same roots.

In G chord position with the capo at the seventh fret

Here's a deconstructed version of the tune that introduces the parts one by one. Start out playing just the bass line with your thumb, and repeat this as many times as necessary to get in the groove. (Notice how similar this part is to a Cuban-style *clave* pattern.) Then introduce the upper picking pattern on the G string alone. When you have the thumb and index finger coordinated, bring in the chord movement and ornaments. When you have this down, you might get entranced and never want to stop playing it!

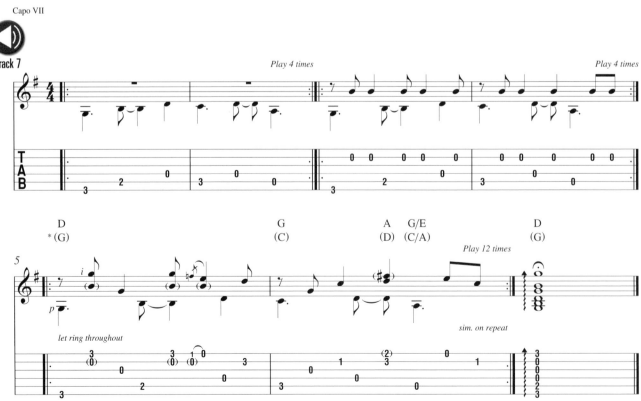

*Symbols in parentheses represent chord names respective to capoed guitar. Symbols above reflect actual sounding chords. Capoed fret is "0" in tab.

THE MIDDLE EAST

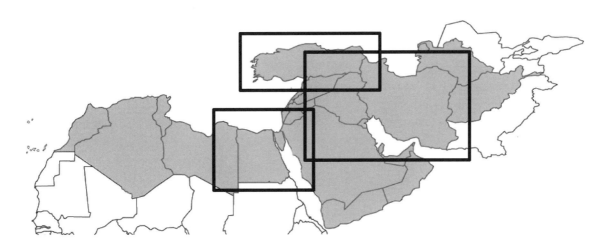

oving northward, we find a part of the world whose cultural history and influence are as rich as its musical styles. Musically speaking, the Middle East includes not only the countries of the Persian Gulf and the Arabian Peninsula, but also the Muslim-influenced areas of North Africa and the Balkans (Turkey, Armenia, etc.).

The very origins of the guitar (and probably all other lute instruments) can be traced back to the Middle East. Ironically—but for good musical reasons—the guitar is not prominent in Middle Eastern music; rather, its predecessors and elder relatives (the oud, tar, saz, etc.) are the main music-making lute instruments. Here we make full use of the similarities and adapt the guitar to the indigenous music.

Where do we begin to describe the music of this part of the world? First of all, it may be impossible to play all varieties of traditional Middle Eastern music on a conventional guitar, because most of it doesn't follow the tempered Western chromatic scale. If Middle Eastern music ever sounds "out of tune," it's because the listener's ears are not accustomed to hearing more than twelve basic pitches within an octave. In the Middle East an octave can contain twenty-four or more different notes, depending on the regional tradition and context. Some of the chosen notes of a piece of music might be a quarter tone away from what you're used to hearing, but once you develop an ear for it, those "off" notes are the gems! For the purposes of this introduction, we won't explore those quarter tones in any great detail, but you can use certain guitar techniques to *allude* to them—without having to remove the frets on your guitar.

Even in Westernized form, most Middle Eastern music has certain elements in common. First, it is more melodic than harmonic. The melody is not traditionally accompanied by chords; rather, a *drone* note—either played or implied—often underscores the melody. Sometimes the drone can shift (or *modulate* to a new tonal center), but within each section of a composition it is static.

Within a piece of music, melodic structure and improvisation is dependent on the *maqam*, a melodic system similar to a scale or mode—but much more complex—that determines the notes, their sequence, and the transitional or ending cadence, among other things. Without the ability to play quarter tones, we can't get deeply into the study of *maqamat*, but we can approximate scales and techniques enough to learn characteristic tunes and styles from a few different traditions.

THE OUD

The *oud* is one of the guitar's great ancestors, the ancient instrument on which the European Medieval/Renaissance lute was based (the word *lute* comes from *l'oud*). The guitar is a kind of cross-breed of the lute and the Baroque *vihuela* (you'll hear more about that in the Spain chapter). The most important difference between the instruments is that the oud has no frets, and that leaves it open to all arrangements of quarter tones in any maqam system. That, along with its deep, mellow tone

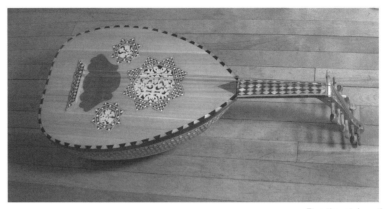
Egyptian-style oud

and portability, helps to make it the most prominent and widely used lute instrument in Middle Eastern music around the globe.

There are many different types of ouds of different sizes and numbers of strings. The most common model has one single low string and five double courses, tuned in any of a number of different pitches and intervals depending on the tradition and the player. Some standards include D–G–A–D–G–C in the Arabic system and E–A–B–E–A–D in the Turkish/Armenian style, but in other instances the single string can be as low as C. The fretless instrument lends itself well to short slides from one note to the next, or slides as note ornaments. The ability of an instrument to glide between notes is prized in the Middle East for being close to the human voice.

The following tune is based on a popular belly dance rhythm (*maqsum*) and a melody roughly in *maqam hijaz*—a sound that is emblematic of "lighter" music from the Arabian Peninsula and beyond. It uses oud-style techniques to navigate and decorate the melody. For the purposes of our arrangement, the guitar's low E string is tuned down to B for a drone note—not a typical key for the oud, but one that accommodates oud stylings on the guitar. On the CD you can hear a low B for reference.

 Low B String

Track 8

Tuning:	drop B (low to high: B–A–D–G–B–E)
Tonality:	mostly in Maqam Hijaz (approximated on the guitar): B – C – D$^\flat$ – E – F$^\sharp$ – G –A($\sharp$)– B (1– $^\flat$2 – 3 – 4 – 5 – $^\flat$6 –($^\flat$)7 – 1)
Picking:	plectrum
Sound:	acoustic steel-string

ALMOST TOUCHING

"Almost Touching" Performance Notes

The A section is grouped in two-measure phrases that consist of a statement and a highly decorated variation. All notes are played in an extended "box" between frets 1 and 5, navigated by sliding from one position to the next. The turnaround in measure 4 is full of short, oud-like slides and slurs (suggested left-hand fingerings are noted above the staff).

The fretting finger mutes the open third string

Section B introduces an upper drone string (or upper pedal point in Western classical terms), common in oud and other Middle Eastern lute styles, and a new melody that adds momentum to the composition. As you slide around the melody, let the edge of your fretting fingers damp the G string between the fretted notes and the open B string, which should be left open to drone above the melody (see photo).

In the B section there is first a melody, then a counter-melody, then a variation of the melody, and finally a more definitive turnaround to bring it back to the A section. This type of motif, punctuated with a *backfalling* move (meas. 8), is typical in Arabic folk and pop music. (You'll also hear some flashier backfalling in the upcoming Turkish example.)

You might have noticed that the melody goes off the beaten path of the maqam with the major 7th note (A$\sharp$) in measures 7–8. This is another tension-building device, released with the return of the A section. It returns again at the end of the fourth A section (meas. 13).

The oud is not traditionally a chordal instrument—nor is Middle Eastern music chord-based—but many modern players have made it more so. When chords are played on it, they usually stack up like the ending chord in this piece: with a close 3rd and no 5th, a warm voicing with lots of space. Again, damp the G string with the edge of a fretting finger.

TURKEY: MUSIC OF THE SAZ

Turkey sits geographically and culturally at the crossroads between Europe and the Middle East, and much of its music rides the fence between Arabic and Greco-Roman Mediterranean flavors. Turkish music has its own brand of maqam, but Western-style tempered scales are also used. The Turkish lute of choice is the *saz*, a long-necked descendant of the original Persian tar. (The Westernized version of the saz is the Greek *bouzouki*.) The typical saz has three or four double courses of strings, tuned in octaves and unison, giving it a shimmering sound not unlike that of a twelve-string guitar, but the strings of the saz are much more flexible and friendly to the very ornamental Turkish style of playing. For the sake of those ornaments, we'll stick to a six-string acoustic on this arrangement.

The piece on the following pages is played mostly in a scale that we in the West call harmonic minor. It looks like a straight minor scale until you get to the 7th, which is major. But that doesn't always hold true here—in upper extensions of the melody, the 7th is minor (the opposite of the previous tune). Here is the way it progresses:

Dan Rein playing the saz

Track 10

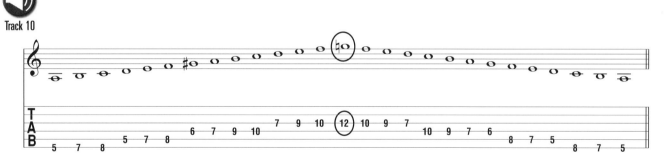

"Üsküdar" is a region of Istanbul, and it's also the name of the following traditional folk dance tune for the saz.

Tuning:	standard
Scale:	A harmonic minor/natural minor hybrid (see above)
Picking:	plectrum
Sound:	acoustic steel-string

ÜSKÜDAR

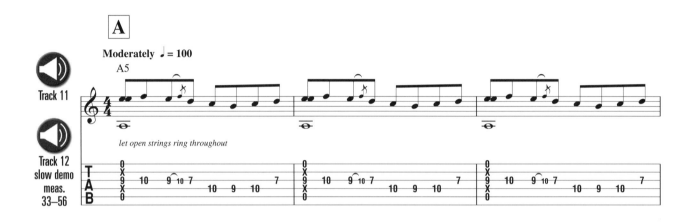

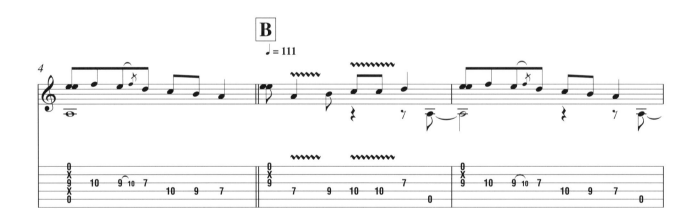

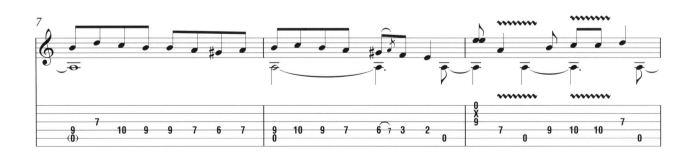

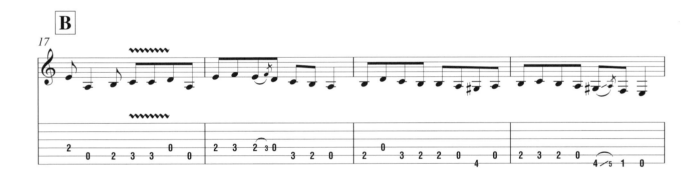

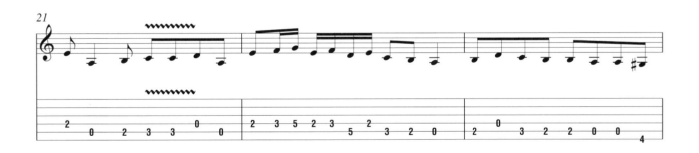

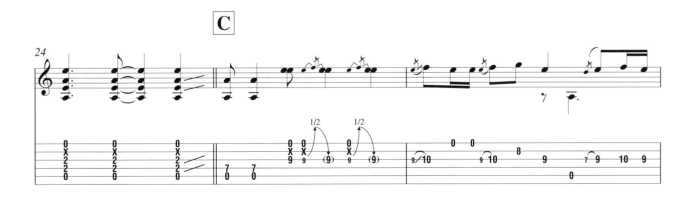

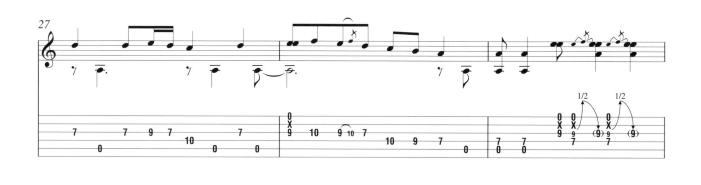

B

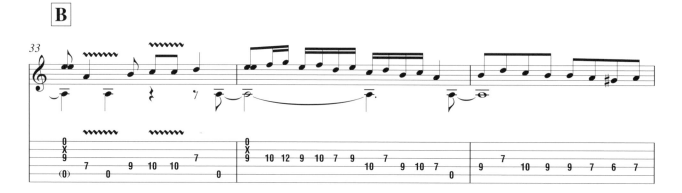

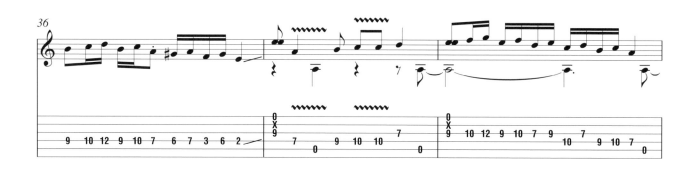

C

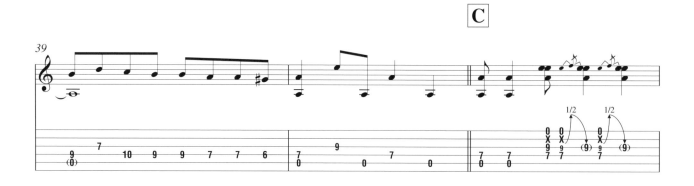

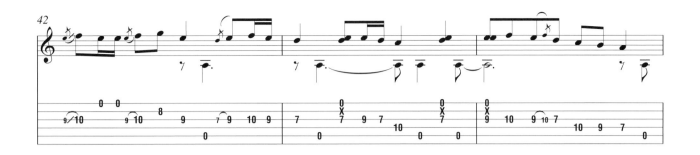

B

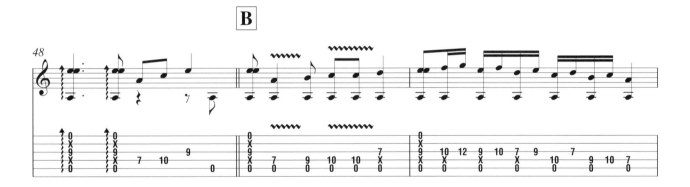

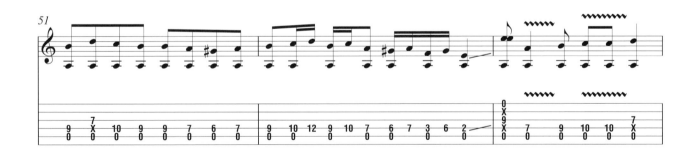

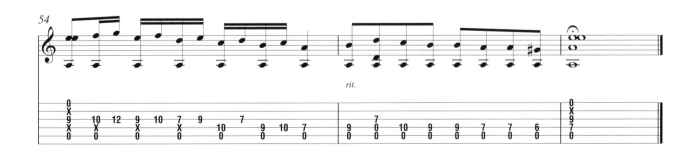

"Üsküdar" Performance Notes

Here we're taking more advantage of open strings to create the drone below the melody, and also unison notes on the higher strings that give the shimmering effects of the saz's double courses and resonant bridge. (This is a technique to be revisited in the next segment on India.)

The essential saz ornament is introduced in measure 1: a hammered grace note that *follows* the main note. Some of us are used to hammering on to the target note from below, or trilling above it with a quick hammer-on and pull-off back to the main note. Consider this a trill that does not return, but instead ends right after it appears (like a quick brush stroke in a line of Turkish calligraphy). Lift your finger off the fret (but not off the string) immediately after you hammer, so the open strings keep ringing while you stop the note and move right on to the next.

The main melody in section B introduces a kind of vibrato that is more than just a shake of the string; it's more like a quick quarter-tone bend-and-repeat, pulled downward to stay out of the way of the open strings. (This holds true wherever vibrato is shown throughout the tune.) You start the melody floating around a box position between frets 7 and 10, but there's a lot of position shifting coming up (mostly to accommodate the open strings). The B section always ends with a common Turkish motif: the tonic note or chord struck three times assertively, sometimes underneath the melody (meas. 12, 24, 40).

Toward the end of the second B section, played an octave lower, comes the first instance of another essential saz frill: backfalling in steps, so that each descending melody note is followed by an upper neighbor, cleanly picked, before moving on to the next (meas. 22). Guitarists from the school of shred rock might be used to playing similar riffs—this is where they come from!

The backfalling recurs more and more as the tune builds momentum—especially on the final B section (measure 49), where the low drone becomes insistent, played under each fully embroidered upper note.

This is where the D string should be damped by the edge of the left-hand index finger as it shifts along the G string, so that the open A string can be picked along with the fast run (see photo). Or, alternately, you can jump up to the D string and play the same notes without the intervening string (just play five frets higher).

The index finger muting the D string

THE PERSIAN TAR

Ancient Persia, now called Iran, is the birthplace of music that influenced not only the Middle East, but the entire musical world. Almost every instrument of the Western orchestra has an ancient Persian prototype, and the Middle Eastern music you've been learning so far has roots in Persian classical styles. Persian classical music has also had a profound influence on the Hindustani music of North India.

The prominent lute of Persia was (and is) the *tar*, a long-necked lute with three double courses of strings, played very much like its offspring, the saz. Tar techniques also transfer to the oud and most other lute instruments of the Middle East.

Without diving into Persian music theory, which has a very complex system all its own, we can take a sample from a *chahar mezrab*—part of a solo performance in which the performer starts playing in a driving rhythm. This one includes picking techniques that are also used on the oud, and follows a *dastgah* (the Persian equivalent of a maqam) that is roughly compatible with the tonality we explored in the previous oud example. Keep in mind that in a genuine *dastgah chahargah*, the 2nd and 6th scale degrees would be sharper by a quarter tone. Consider this the tiniest sample of what the tar and Persian classical music are all about.

Tuning:	standard
Tonality:	Dastgah Chahargah (approximated on the guitar): B – C – D♯ – E – F♯ – G – A(♯)– B (1 – ♭2 – 3 – 4 – 5 – ♭6 – (♭)7 – 1)
Picking:	flatpick (see suggested picking patterns below the staff)
Sound:	acoustic steel-string

DASTGAH CHAHARGAH

Track 13

Shuffle feel ♩ = 134

Play 3 times

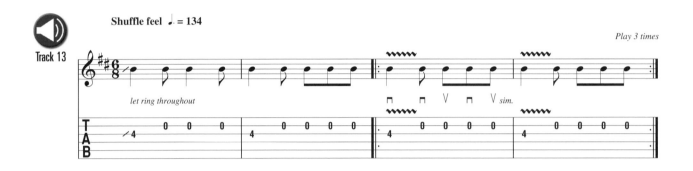

let ring throughout

sim.

%

Play 4 times

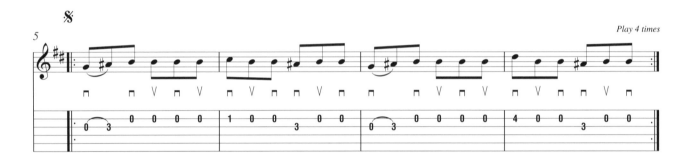

5

To Coda ⊕

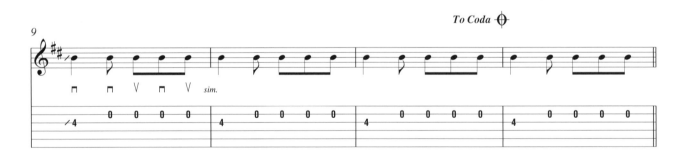

9

sim.

13

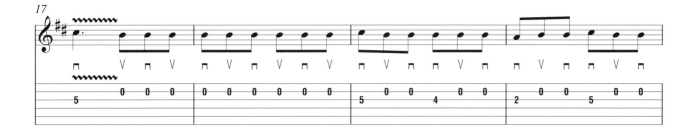

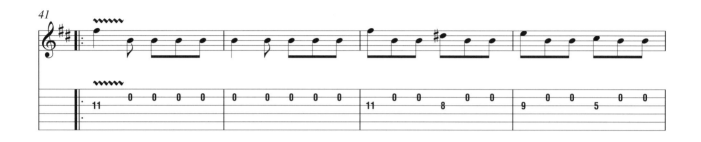

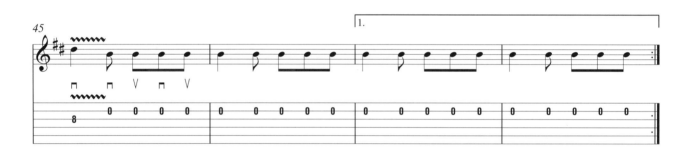

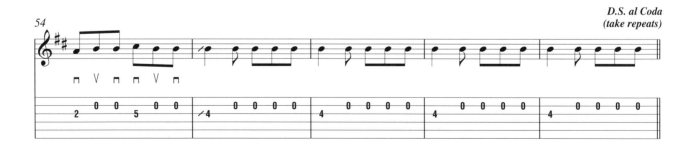

"Dastgah Chahargah" Performance Notes

This serves as a snapshot of the kind of picking techniques that are used in all manner of Middle Eastern lute music. Suggested picking patterns are shown under the staff wherever they might be useful.

You can begin with the idea that you're alternate-picking eighth notes, starting with a downstroke on beat 1 of every measure, and strategically missing the upstroke wherever there's a pause for a quarter note. Coming from a guitarist's perspective, you may already have this technique down by heart. But when you start alternating fretted notes with the open B string (meas. 5), straight alternate-picking might have you jumping awkwardly from string to string. That's where I find that my right hand wants to approach every fretted note as a down-stroke—and that's just what most oud players do with this kind of line. Even though it feels like a stutter at first, it accents the appropriate notes and gives you the clean, percussive sound that's called for.

The same kind of picking applies in the B section, when an increasingly complex melody builds against the droning open string. Similar to the Turkish example, what's shown as vibrato is more like a quick quarter-tone bend-and-release of the fretted note on the 1—a kind of soulful sting.

Melodically speaking, you'll notice how the 7th scale degree is major at the outset (A♯ in meas. 5) and minor on the way down (A♮ in meas. 20, 36, and 54). See a pattern developing here? The oud/belly-dance tune had the opposite approach, and "Üsküdar" had the minor 7th appearing in upper extensions. Dastgah and maqam systems often have melodic twists like this, as well as a kind of prescribed ornamentation that is appropriate to specific notes and the way they are approached. You'll see more of this, applied in a very different way, in the section on Indian music.

ASIA

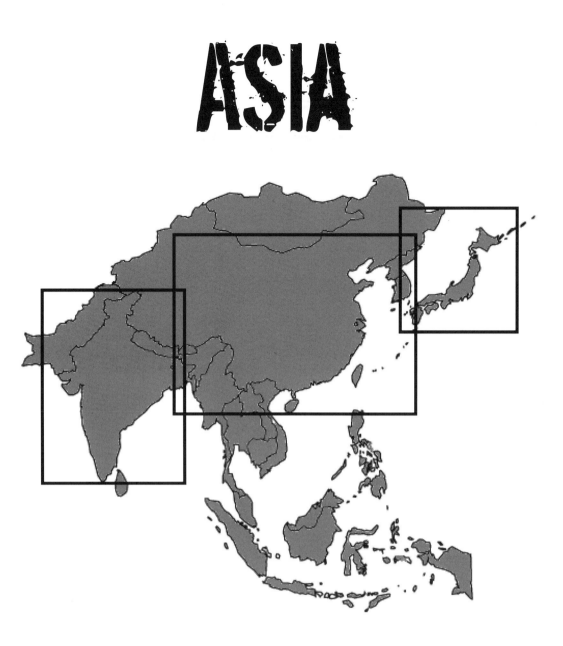

Here is another vast and musically diverse part of the world in which the guitar is not the traditional star player. It's far from absent these days, however, and you will see that the earlier Asian offspring of the lute family thrive in endlessly beautiful varieties. The guitar has the capability to cop lots of these other instruments' licks—even those that have very little in common with it. We'll use it here to explore the sounds of some of its ancient Asian relatives. Be warned: this will involve some new and happily challenging techniques.

For our purposes Asia includes the Indian subcontinent, much of China, and Japan. These are considered some of the most distinct and independent musical places on the Eastern map, although the subtle colors of Asian music are nearly endless in their variety.

INDIA: THE SOUND OF INFINITY

The Indian subcontinent is rich with diverse and complex styles of music, some of which are closely related to the Middle East, but each with its own character. In the classical realm, we distinguish the Northern *(Hindustani)* and Southern *(Carnatic)* styles, and within those divisions there are many "lighter" and "heavier" subgenres.

Indian classical music is among the most complex and expressive art forms in the world, emphasizing improvisation within a system that is at least as methodical as Western classical music (which often seems rigid and lifeless in comparison) and has the soul and artistry of jazz. A thorough education in the deepest forms of Indian classical music would take a lifetime—or three. We'll sample a couple of the lighter styles here, and some uniquely Indian, guitar-friendly techniques.

In popular culture, the instrument most commonly associated with India has been the Hindustani *sitar* (thanks mostly to Ravi Shankar's association with the West). In fact there are slide guitars, mandolins, violins, and all varieties of ancient and modern lute instruments in Indian classical music.

The *veena*, a predecessor of the sitar, is the traditional lute of choice in the South Indian tradition. The following excerpt from a Carnatic *kriti* (a light classical song form) showcases some of the veena's trademarks, including wide bends and vibrato (accommodated by scalloped frets), slides, rhythmic displacement, and plucked drone strings. You'll hear part of the main *Pallavi* section of the tune, when the main melody is established and before the improv gets too intense.

Nirmala Rajasekar plays the veena

In Indian music almost all notes are ornamented, often according to the *raga* used. A raga (or *rag*) is a kind of melodic framework, much more than just a scale. It often has different ascending and descending forms, an association with a season, time of day, or deity, and specific ornaments, among other things. "Anuragamuleni" is in *Rag Sarasvati*, which has five ascending notes (plus the octave) and six descending. Here is the rag with E as the tonic. Notice how the D note is approached on the way down:

Track 14

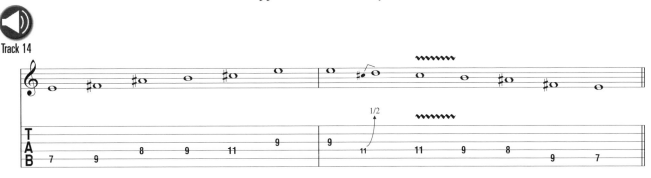

Some guitarists, like John McLaughlin, have played guitars with scalloped (concave or dipped) frets to achieve veena-style bends and vibrato. We can get similar results on this example with light bendable strings, fairly low action on the fretboard, and strong, accurate fingers.

Tuning:	standard
Scale/Key:	Rag Sarasvati in E (see previous page)
Picking:	fingers or hybrid
Sound:	acoustic steel-string guitar, or electric with a clean tone

ANURAGAMULENI
(EXCERPT)

Traditional Carnatic

*Key signature denotes Rag Sarasvati in E.

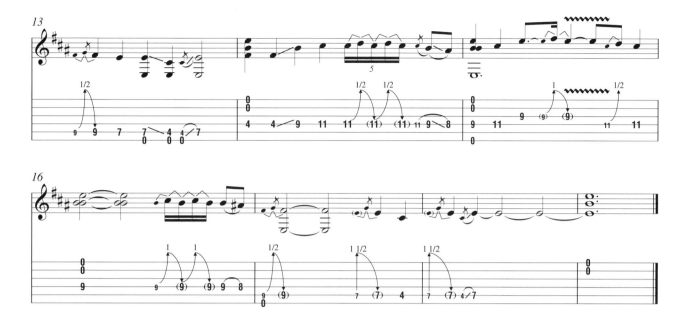

"Anuragamuleni" Performance Notes

This example was fingerpicked with the thumb, index, and middle fingers (for our purposes the fingering is not strict). Wherever you hear open strings plucked along with melody notes, they're playing the role of the veena's plucked drone strings. The drone is an essential element here, hence the requisite *tanpura* sound you hear in the background (a staple sound in all Indian classical music).

What does this talk of drones mean for you as a guitarist? Since we're in the key of E, you have the open first, second, and sixth strings to work with. The open low E marks the beginning of each main four-measure phrase (meas. 1, 5, and 9), and the others come in to reinforce some key melody notes. (Many Indian instruments have *sympathetic* drone strings that do this automatically, ringing in sympathy along with the main strings.) So you often have a unison note picked along with the melody and ringing out while its counterpart bends or slides around. Let the open strings keep ringing as much as possible.

Just as important as the notes you see on the page are the "anti-notes" in between them—the bends and slides—and how they are executed. For the sake of strength and accuracy, follow the golden rule of string bending: for bends on (the lower-sounding) strings 4, 5, or 6, pull downward toward the earth; for (the higher-sounding) strings 1–3, push upward toward the sky. The second phrase of the main melody (meas. 2, 4, 6, and 8) has the kind of fast whole-step bend-release-and-repeat that's typical on the veena and sitar. If bending isn't your forté, work up to it slowly, and make sure your strings are light enough not to mangle your fingers.

The melody gets varied and busier around measure 9, with a precise unison pre-bend and slide, then more ornaments and vibrato, which should be wide and fast throughout. Again, think of the vibrato in this piece as a movement between a note and another note a quarter-tone above it. Indian music theory recognizes not only the same twelve chromatic semitones that are used in Western scales, but also ten more *microtones* that apply in ornaments like this. A veena guru would notice if your target pitch is off, but we won't get quite so involved here…

This excerpt of "Anuragamuleni" winds down with wide bends on the A string, resolving with a slide up to the tonic E note (meas. 17–18). In the full kriti, this break would signal the beginning of the *Anupallavi* section, during which the artists improvise off the main pattern. You are encouraged to seek out opportunities to hear this happening for real and experience the interplay between the soloist and percussionist.

North Indian music has much in common with music of the South, the main differences being attributed to a direct Persian influence. Deep Hindustani classical music tends to have more of a meditative quality, but flashy virtuosity abounds among the players. The following tune shows many dynamic elements of the lighter Hindustani genres (*dhun, dadra, ghazal,* etc.), including repeated melodic phrases that create polyrhythmic motifs. The *tabla* drums work closely with the melody instrument on these breaks.

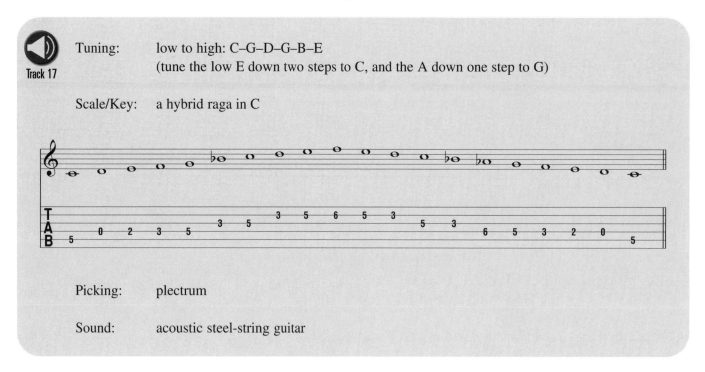

Track 17

Tuning: low to high: C–G–D–G–B–E
                 (tune the low E down two steps to C, and the A down one step to G)

Scale/Key: a hybrid raga in C

Picking: plectrum

Sound: acoustic steel-string guitar

KHAN SONG

Traditional Hindustani

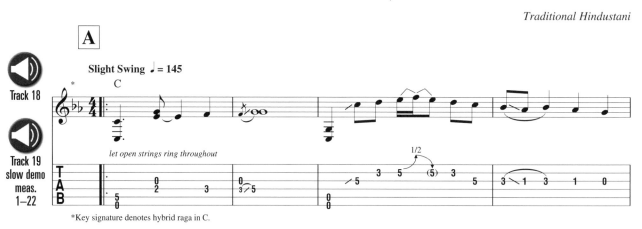

*Key signature denotes hybrid raga in C.

"Khan Song" Performance Notes

With the two lowest strings tuned down, we have a low C tonic note and the 5th, G, to reinforce the drone. Open G and E strings played "inside" the melody fill the role of plucked or sympathetic drones, as in the previous Carnatic example. Here we're using more slides than bends to cover the *meend*, those glides from one pitch to the next that touch on the microtones between the notes.

The opening main melody is grouped in repeating two-measure phrases. The repeating one-measure phrase in measures 12–14 is a *tihai* ("tee-high"), a cadential pattern repeated three times and calculated to end on beat 1. (You will hear a lot of these, improvised, in Hindustani classical music.) What follows in section B is a bit more complex: a repeated motif that is cycled in different registers *and meters*, superimposed in such a way that you can count in 4 all the way through and end up on beat 1—but what is played is more like three measures of 7/4, followed by four measures of 5/8 and a climactic pause leading back into the main melody (see the brackets above the staff). It's better felt than counted, but it sure is satisfying to know what mathematical wonders you're accomplishing when you play this.

Techniques throughout this tune are sitar-like, as in the repeated slides in measures 9–14, and the box shifting during the odd-against-even measures of section B. Play the first seven-count riff between frets 5 and 3 on the G and D strings, then shift your entire hand up to play the next, and so on (suggested left-hand fingerings are noted on the staff). Each falls into a different "box" of the same scale. Sitar (and other Indian lute) playing tends to be more horizontal than vertical, with the left hand shifting quickly across one string—often while another drones underneath it. The same kind of technique is used to full effect in the Turkish example "Üsküdar," betraying some of the Persian influence in both traditions.

CHINA: MUSIC OF THE PIPA

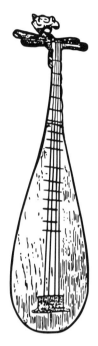

The guitar has many ancient Chinese cousins, most of them evolved from early Persian prototypes. One of the most versatile, dynamic, and popular is the *pipa*, a four-stringed, pear-shaped, fretted lute with a thin wooden body and a unique design that accommodates virtuoso techniques: ultra-wide string bends, harmonics, percussive strumming, sound effects, and a distinctive style of tremolo fingerpicking creating by "flicking" the strings in a fan-like motion with the *backs* of the fingers, one after the other, to get a smooth, fluttering sound.

We won't pretend that this is easily done on the guitar (though you're welcome to prove otherwise), but we can get similar results with slightly more familiar picking techniques. Just be prepared for a satisfying challenge!

One of China's most beloved tunes for pipa is an arrangement of a folk dance melody from the Yi tribe, a minority group from Sichuan province. A lyrical theme is developed in dynamic Chinese style with varying degrees of subtlety. Bends and vibrato are essential to the feel.

Gao Hong playing the pipa

Tuning:	standard
Scale/Key:	A minor, with emphasis on minor pentatonic notes
Picking:	fingers or hybrid
Sound:	acoustic steel- or nylon-string guitar (with bendable light-guage strings)—extra-light steel strings were used on the recording

SONG OF THE YI PEOPLE
(EXCERPT)

Traditional

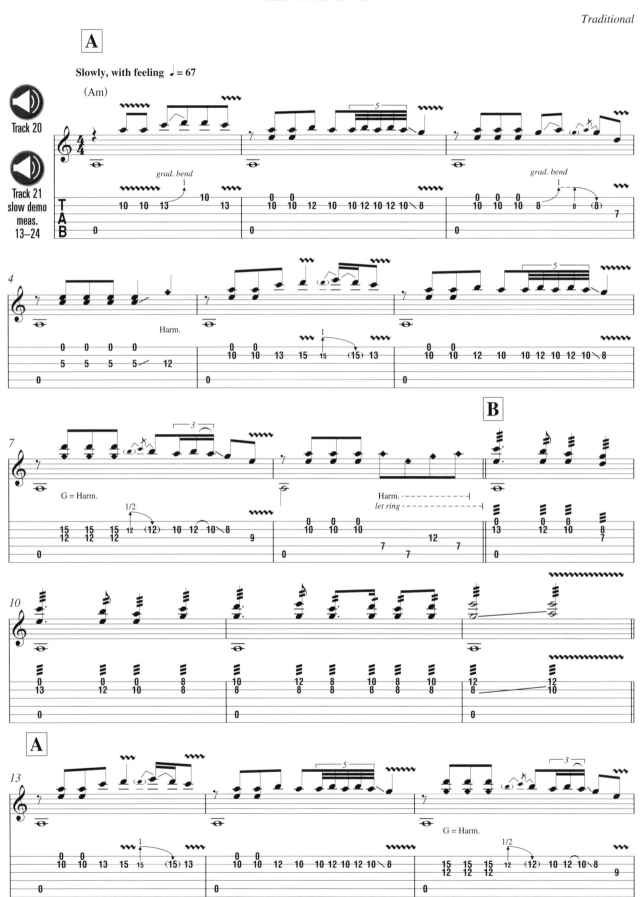

"Song of the Yi People" Performance Notes

Much of this piece could be approximated with a pick and a very fast wrist, but I use a very alternative finger-style technique that stays true to the pipa feel. The tremolo picking (beginning in section B) is covered with a fast down-and-up flutter of the middle finger, while the thumb plucks bass notes on the open string. This results in a sound very close to that of the pipa player's fan-picking technique and all its subtleties.

Pipa-style tremolo

If you do use a pick, you will need to go hybrid (use pick and fingers) every time you pick a bass note while tremolo-picking over it: your pick hits the bass note while your middle and third fingers reach over to pluck the B and E strings; then the pick immediately jumps to the higher strings to continue fluttering the melody. However, if you go pickless and let your middle finger do the fluttering (and it cooperates), the thumb is free to pluck bass notes with less distractions. Use whichever technique your fingers prefer.

When the bass notes start moving in 5ths under a changing melody in section C, sometimes the best choice is a harmonic (meas. 17); at other times the left hand hammers on the 5th (meas. 18, 22, 24) to give the right-hand thumb a well-deserved break.

The fast, expressive vibrato here is intrinsic in Chinese music. Pipa players do this with a left-hand vibrato technique that is more of an up-and-down finger pull than a side-to-side wrist-rocking motion. (Rocking your wrist blues-style would make your finger run into another string that might have to sound while the main one is wiggling.) Listen to the slow demo and take your time developing these delicate techniques.

JAPAN: MUSIC OF THE KOTO

Classical composers of the modern avant-garde movement have been heavily influenced by the traditional court music of Japan. Its distinct sounds and tonalities have what many in the West consider a haunting quality, and its structure, often based on repetition and variation, belies its complexity and players' discipline.

Most Japanese chamber instruments are unique adaptations of ancient Chinese prototypes. Perhaps the most distinctively Japanese stringed instrument is the *koto*, a large, plucked thirteen-stringed zither with very harp-like qualities. There are particular sounds and playing styles associated with the koto—bends, pick scrapes, glissandos, etc.—as well as a pair of archetypal Japanese scales. Articulation is very important in the chamber music of Japan—often more so than melodic development. If some Western listeners find Far East music melodically boring, that's because they're not listening to the way the notes are played!

This brings us back to an important point. Anyone can learn the notes associated with an ethnic style of music. Play it like a guitarist, and you'll sound like a guitarist trying half-heartedly to cop a koto lick! The essence of a musical style is not only in the notes and sound; the way a note is ornamented makes all the difference. To illustrate, here is a straight transcription of a melody in the *In* scale, a pentatonic (five-note) scale that is emblematic of Japanese music:

Track 22

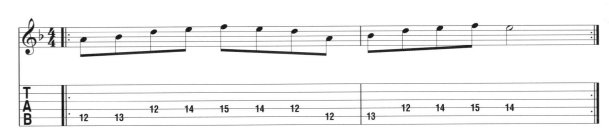

Now here it is played with the koto feel, using a combination of harmonics and fretted notes to capture the instrument's harp-like sustain, and strategic pre-bends that mirror the behind-the-bridge string-bending technique of koto players. Listen to the difference on the CD.

Track 22
(cont.)

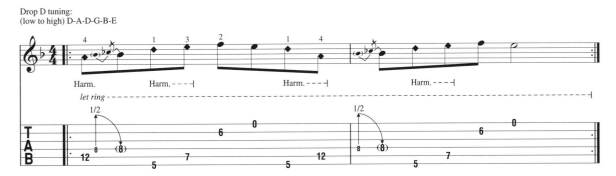

Using techniques like these, a guitarist can really capture the expressive power of a traditional piece of music. "Rokudan" is one of the most popular pieces in the koto repertoire. The techniques in this guitar arrangement of its first movement make it faithful to the spirit of the original.

Track 23

Tuning:	drop D (low to high, D–A–D–G–B–E)
Scale/Key:	Yona Nuki minor scale in G (G minor with 4th and 7th omitted): $1 - 2 - \flat3 - 5 - \flat6$ $G - A - B\flat - D - E\flat$
Picking:	fingers or hybrid
Sound:	acoustic steel- or nylon-string guitar (with bendable light-gauge strings)
Special technique:	harmonics combined with fretted notes—you'll see a diamond notehead and "Harm." above or below the staff, depending on which note is to be played as a harmonic

ROKUDAN NO SHIRABE
(EXCERPT)

Yatsuhashi Kengyo

Track 24

Track 25
slow demo
meas.
3–5,
9–10

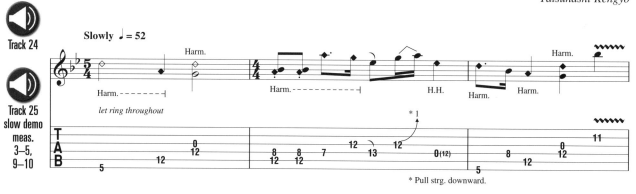

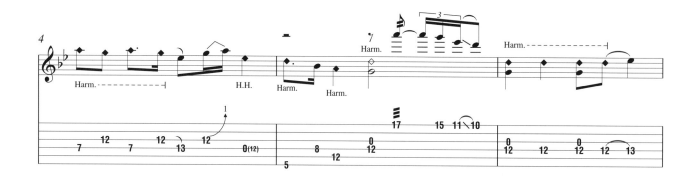

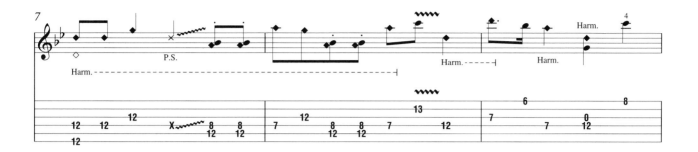

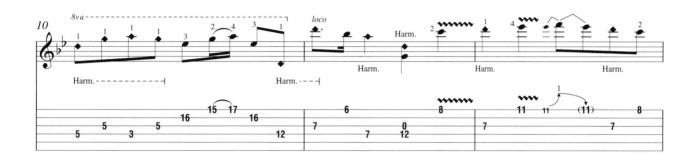

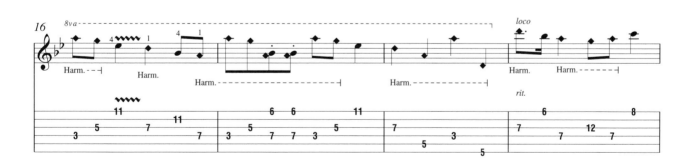

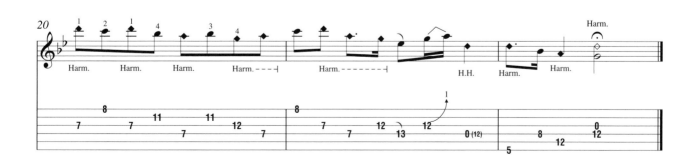

"Rokudan" Performance Notes

Were you warned that this might be tricky? Good. Sensitivity is the key to playing all these combined harmonics and fretted/bent notes. Keep any unused left-hand fingers floating over the fretboard, so that each note sustains into the next, except when muting those dissonant staccato dyads (meas. 2, 7, 8, 15, 17) that serve as punctuating dots. Watch for these and other places where harmonics and natural notes sound together, and know which fingers to use for long jumps across the fretboard (suggested fingerings are noted). There are also some quick *artificial* (or harp) harmonics played exclusively with the right hand. The standard way to play these is with your index finger touching the string node above the desired fret while your thumb plucks. I find it more convenient to reverse this, touching the node with my thumb while picking with the finger; this way I don't have to re-orient my hand to regular picking position after playing the harp harmonic (as in the photo below).

Playing a harp harmonic

Measure 1 has an odd five beats, establishing the theme with extra space in reflective Japanese style. After the first "dot dot" comes a pair of natural harmonics, then a hammered E♭ on fret 13 followed by a *downward* whole-step bend of the G string, fret 12 (hence the light strings). Holding the bent note, reach over with your right hand to pluck a harp harmonic directly above it (see photo). If your strings are not this bendable, just slide from fret 12 to 14 on the G string.

Motives and techniques like these recur in variation throughout this arrangement, along with a couple of frills. The little flutter of notes at the end of measure 5 is a simulated koto glissando, played with the same flutter-picking technique that was used in the Chinese pipa tune. (Make sure you don't mute the A and D strings, which should continue sustaining through the fill.)

The ascending pick scrape in measure 7 is another koto technique, here played with the thumbnail. When the main theme goes up an octave, there's a long jump across the fretboard in measure 10. You're covering thirteen strings with six, so be patient with yourself!

WESTERN EUROPE

The classical guitar traditions of Western Europe and the Americas were built upon refinements of lute music that sprouted up all over Europe from the Middle Ages onward. Medieval trade, wars, and diplomacy helped bring the lute into Western European consciousness, and the courtly music-makers of later years took to re-creating it in their own tempered musical image. We'll look to Spain for the origins of modern guitar music, then go upward and outward to explore some very creative uses of the guitar in the Celtic music of the British isles.

SPAIN: A GUITAR IS BORN

The classical-style guitar pretty much as we know it, a fretted, tempered lute with six strings tuned E–A–D–G–B–E, evolved in Spain and/or Portugal during the baroque period of the seventeenth and eighteenth centuries. Its lute predecessor had traveled there from the Middle East via the Moors and begun to take on a guitar-like appearance during the 1300s. The basic guitar design was slowly adapted to the needs of burgeoning Western classical music. (A close relative, the *vihuela*, had previously been the Spanish lute of choice and continued being used throughout the baroque period.)

Naturally, the land that spawned the guitar also brought some of the most complex and beautiful music ever played on it. Some of the earliest Spanish guitar music ever put on paper was done so by the composer Gaspar Sanz, who

Vihuela (left) and baroque guitar

compiled and transcribed a collection of Spanish dances for his *guitarra española* (Spanish guitar) method in 1674. The most legendary of them, "Canarios," became a musical emblem of Spain, as well as source material for much later classical composers, most notably Joaquín Rodrigo.

Sanz's arrangement of "Canarios" was influenced by Italian and Northern European baroque styles, but the original themes are purely Spanish. An excerpt is arranged here that combines classical-style fingerpicking with more distinctly Iberian overtones, some of which hint at the later movement known as *flamenco*, a subject for another book or three. You'll also notice the melodic and rhythmic similarities between this and later Latin American styles.

Tuning:	standard
Scale/Key:	D major
Picking:	fingerstyle
Sound:	acoustic nylon-string guitar

CANARIOS DE-CLASSICIZED

Variations on a theme of Gaspar Sans

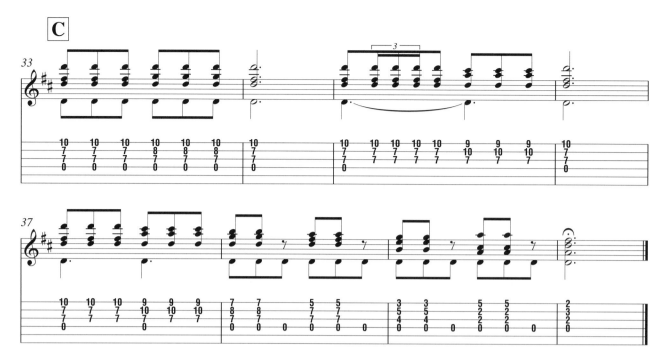

"Canarios" Performance Notes

If you're not familiar with classical-style fingerpicking, the only strict rule to follow here is that the thumb plays lower notes, just as in most of the fingerpicking examples you've seen so far in this book. As for the melody, serious classical players tend to alternate the index and middle finger—but you're under no obligation to do it completely "by the book." Sometimes it's convenient to alternate between thumb and index finger, as in the downward E–D–C♯ run of measure 2—you'll need your thumb in that area anyway, to pluck the open G string in meas. 2. You're encouraged to alternate fingers or finger/thumb as much as possible, for practical reasons (that makes it easier to play fast), but the rest is (mostly) up to you.

Notice how the bass notes follow just behind the melody in strategic parts of sections A and B; this is in the contrapuntal baroque style of the time. These passages call for some delicate playing that lets the upper and lower voices be heard evenly. Things get more unorthodox later on.

The original manuscript of "Canarios," from which this bit was expanded, was much more subdued and classicized; there was no tapping on the guitar or heavy strumming with the fingernails. Here it's given a little more of the expressive verve that typifies Spanish music, with the idea that Sanz's transcription was a refinement. (Interpreters of early Iberian vocal music have done a similar thing in performance.) You'll also get a taste of some of the dynamism of Spanish guitar playing.

The first major departure is in the first B section (meas. 10), where we start working in a bit of the technique later known as *rasgueado* ("raked"), a fast flamenco-style strumming technique accomplished with the backs of the fingernails. Here, just flick the chords with the nails. More of this happens in section C: measure 17 is simply strumming down and up with the nails; meas. 19 is one downward strum, followed by a fan-like motion using all four fingers one at a time (from pinky to index, each finger flicks the strings one after the other). In between these strums we have thumb taps on the body of the guitar. The chords of section C fall in a tuneful and rhythmic pattern that has been used everywhere as an emblem of Hispanic music, from American classical composers to Mexican mariachi bands.

The next embellishment comes at the end of the second B section (meas. 31): a fast run of mostly pull-offs (pick just the first note on each string) to take you back into the strumming section.

You'll notice that the low E string sits out the whole tune, because the baroque guitar of Sanz's time had only five double courses of unison strings, A–D–G–B–E. If you're burning to use the low string, try tuning it down to D and adding it to the strumming effects of section C (but first, learn the tune as-is).

IRELAND: CELTIC GUITAR

The guitar was not a traditional instrument in the Celtic traditions of Ireland and the greater British Isles. In fact, as of this writing, Celtic melodies have only been played on the guitar for about the last few decades! Its earlier use as an accompaniment instrument was sparse, and among the more staunch folk traditionalists it is still not fully accepted. Amazing, then, that a uniquely Celtic style of guitar playing and system of tunings has arisen to become so widespread and influential in the world of folk music, not to mention rock and pop.

Celtic music is melodic by nature, and traditionally played on solo instruments like fiddle, flute, harp, or pipes. In the latter case, harmonic accompaniment consisted of just a drone note. When guitarists started accompanying traditional tunes, they came up with creative ways to produce the drone along with chords. First, tuning the low E string down to D facilitated a low drone that was well suited to the qualities of traditional music. But it didn't end there.

Instruments like the tin whistle, the Celtic harp, and the uilleann pipes are *modal*—their playing key is fixed by their design, allowing them to play only in a few certain keys, the main ones being D and G. Detuning the guitar further gives us, low to high, D–A–D–G–A–D, which easily supports the keys of D, G, and A, effectively turning the guitar into a modal, yet versatile, instrument. DADGAD has become the "alternative standard" tuning in Celtic music—and it's easy to remember by name, no less.

Interpreting Celtic music on solo guitar often means playing the parts of multiple instruments, covering melody, bass, and rhythm. The Celtic guitarist is also trying to imitate the playing techniques of those other instruments, whether it's the drone of the pipes, the fluid melodies and double stops of the fiddle, or the ringing open strings of the harp. All of the above is accomplished in DADGAD with a combination of fluid fretwork and inventive picking by the "traditional outsiders" of Celtic guitar.

Here is one such guitar interpretation of a traditional *jig*, a variety of dance tune that is felt in 6/8 time (as opposed to the 4/4 *reel* and the 2/4 *hornpipe*). In this swinging compound meter, each of the two main beats is divided into three. "Jerry's Beaver Hat" is one of many documented Irish jigs with interesting names of unknown origin. (No beavers were harmed in the making of this recording.)

Track 28

Tuning:	low to high, D–A–D–G–A–D
Scale/Key:	D major
Picking:	plectrum
Sound:	acoustic steel-string guitar

JERRY'S BEAVER HAT

Traditional Jig

*Play A on repeat only.

"Jerry's Beaver Hat" Performance Notes

This tune has two main sections, within which there is a lot of room for subtle variation. The main theme (section A) has a four-measure "question" phrase ending on an unresolved E note (not counting the low drone), then an "answer" that does resolve to the tonic D. On the repeat, the low open fifth string (A) is added in measure 4 for subtle, but important, forward harmonic movement—effectively changing the bass note to the V chord. Part B is likewise in four-measure Q&A form; the resolution this time is in the form of a decorative run that suspends the resolution until the last eighth note.

All this is punctuated and underscored with low drone notes and open upper strings. These can be somewhat arbitrary, privy to the whims of the artiste, as long as they don't clash with the melody. You'll notice that in this tuning, the tonic (D) is available for your droning pleasure on three open strings, the 5th (A) on two, and the 4th (G) even adds a friendly sus4 sound when it's hit during the B section. Use that one sparingly, and it will have more spine-tingling effects when it appears.

Picking this piece involves strategically missing the strings whenever there's a pull-off to play, and jumping strings occasionally as in the A section (meas. 1–2 and 5–6). There is no strict alternate picking pattern to follow, but keep the swinging 6/8 feel happening—often the pick falls in a shuffle pattern while notes are hammered and pulled in between as eighth notes. Keep it fluid and steady.

Another advantage of DADGAD tuning is that it creates nice, symmetrical box shapes on the fretboard. Your fingers can sit in the same D major box, between frets 2 and 4, until the B section. Then there's a little finger stretching on the high D string, to create a very pipe-like effect (especially when the second string is hit along with the melody). Warning: the pull-offs on this string might threaten to pull the string off the lower edge of the neck (and create a note you don't want) if you pull too hard.

The fast riff that turns the tune around in meas. 15–16 is back in the D major box—a piece of cake as long as it's in the groove.

THE AMERICAS

We won't be learning "Home on the Range" here, but we do owe homage to some of the guitar traditions that grew up in the cultures of the greater "New World," particularly Latin America and the U.S. Pacific island state of Hawai'i. The latter area is smaller and easier to pigeonhole stylistically, but in covering Latin America's guitar traditions, we'll have to pick and choose among those that have historically had the most prominent and distinctive guitars: Mexican mariachi, Brazilian jazz, and the Andean folk of South America.

THE ANDES

The Andean music groups you might hear at art fairs and events across the U.S., sometimes playing pan-flute covers of contemporary pop songs, have necessarily changed with the times and the marketplace, and they have also happily managed to keep their native sound and songs intact. Their musical origins are among the Inca, Aymara, and other ancient Andean civilizations of Ecuador, Peru, Bolivia, Argentina, and Chile. The traditional music is an intriguing mix of those native traditions and colonial Hispanic influence. The signature wind and string sounds have an ancient quality that sounds like the voices of the mountains.

The sounds of the *quena* (cane notched flute), *antara* (pan pipes), *charango* (small lute originally made from an armadillo shell, pictured), and guitar came into vogue as the signature sound of the *nueva canción* "new song" movement of the 1960s through 1990s. A popular adaptation of the traditional tune *El Condor Pasa* (by Simon and Garfunkel) helped spread Andean sounds in the Northern Hemisphere, but that was just one side of the music.

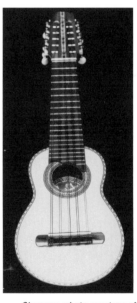

*Charango photo courtesy of
Manuel Navarro*

The *bailecito* ("little dance") is a principal genre of traditional music that showcases the more energetic side of Andes music. The fixed form of the tune gives cues to the dancers it accompanies, relying on rhythmic interplay between the guitar and the *charango*, which was an indigenous version of a small lute brought by the Spanish conquistadors. In the following arrangement, both the guitar and charango parts are arranged for nylon-string guitar. (No armadillos were harmed in the making of this recording!)

Tuning:	standard
Scale/Key:	E minor
Picking:	plectrum
Sound:	guitars 1 and 2: nylon-string acoustic
	guitar 1: (ideally) neck should be accessible up to frets 14–17

BAILECITOS

Traditional

Guitar 2 Chords

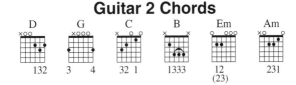

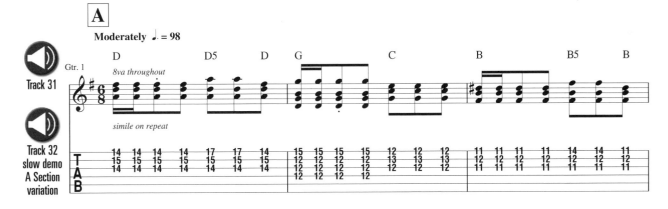

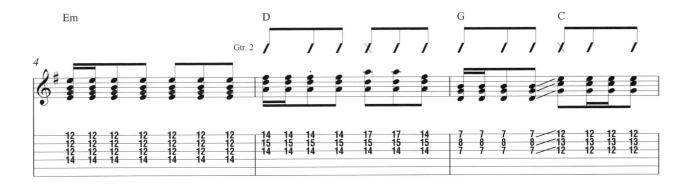

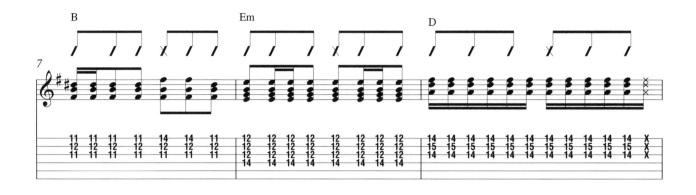

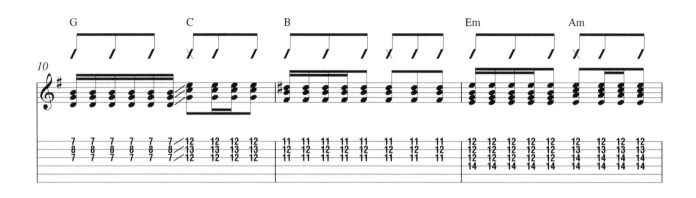

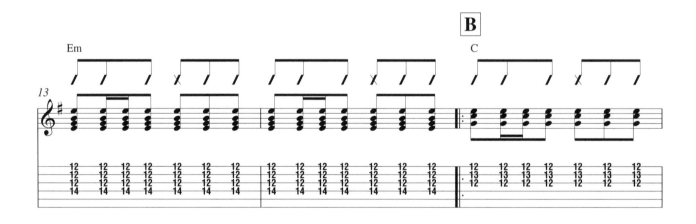

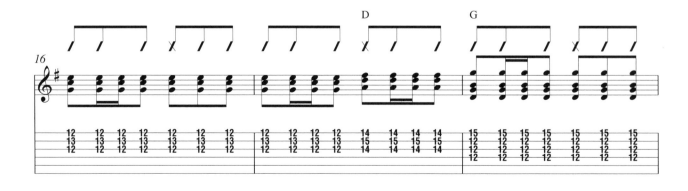

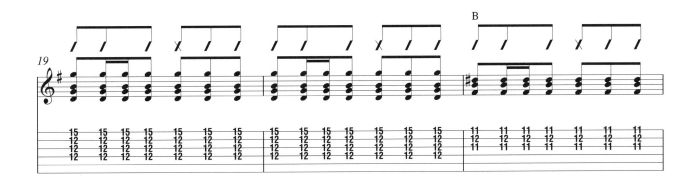

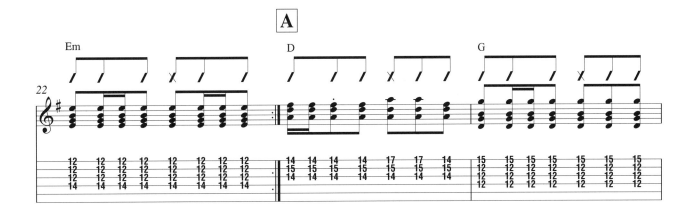

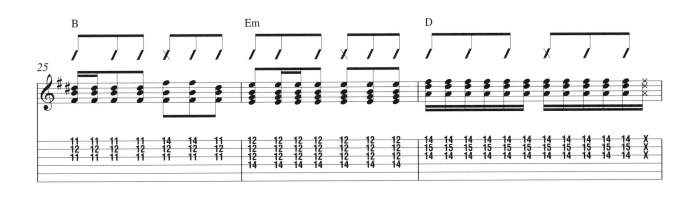

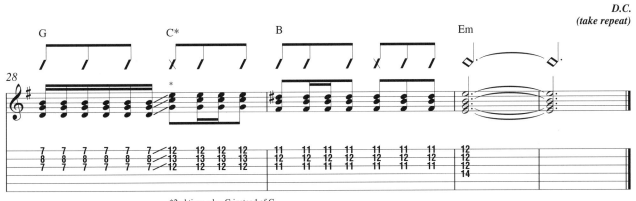

*2nd time, play G instead of C.

"Bailecitos" Performance Notes

This is an interesting fusion of native and Hispanic influences, as is Andean music in general. Rhythmically, it's very Hispanic, but the progressions and techniques are unique to South America.

The opening chord progression (D–G–C–B–Em) has some very adventurous movement compared to many of the popular Latino folk standards, which generally stick to I–IV–V and similar formulas. Here it's hard to pinpoint the tonal center until it settles into Em. This makes the B section more climactic when it moves to C. Compare this with the chord progression of the popular tune "El Condor Pasa," which is much simpler, but also centers around Em and modulates at the bridge to C–G, finally settling back into Em—a very Andean formula, made more complex on "Bailecitos" with a lot more chord movement, not to mention energetic strumming and rhythmic interplay.

This arrangement of the charango part (Guitar 1) calls for reaching up to the nether regions of the fretboard to play a fourteenth-fret D major triad, among other things. If your guitar doesn't accommodate this, it's an opportunity for you to find different voicings for the chords you can't reach. You'll notice that the part slides around a bit later in the song, charango-style. This arrangement is casual; it's no problem to play a different voicing, skip a strum now and then for effect, or to go totally frenetic—as long as your chords fall in the right spaces rhythmically.

One tricky technique is muting between strums to get a choppy effect, as in the first chord of the intro: you quickly strum down-up-down, pick your left hand off the fretboard (but not off the strings) for a quick mute, then strum the chord again—all in the space of half a measure. Continue simile, but let it vary—that's part of the beauty of this tune.

Guitar 2 is more static and supportive, slapping the strings percussively in between strums (this is a technique you'll hear in variation all over Latin America, particularly in the upcoming mariachi tune). The slap on beat 4 helps keep the beat steady on a pattern that might otherwise feel awkward.

A testament to the uniqueness of the "Bailecitos" is that it has been classicized in different forms for solo piano and guitar (most notably by the Argentinian composer Carlos Guastavino). In its subdued classical form it only vaguely resembles the original but hangs on to its Andean spirit.

BRAZILIAN BOSSA NOVA

The many different styles of Brazilian music include *samba*, the groundbreaking style that started in the early 1900s, and *bossa nova*, which grew from samba and became the sound most associated with Brazilian jazz guitar as it is heard in the northern hemisphere. During the 1960s, guitarists and composers like Luiz Bonfá, João Gilberto, and Antonio Carlos Jobim helped popularize bossa nova in the world of pop and jazz, where it is still prominent and influential today. Bossa nova is usually played in a moderate 4/4 feel, while samba is felt in a more energetic 2. Here we'll take a closer look at bossa—which generally has more syncopation between chords and bass notes—understanding that the patterns can be applied to samba if you choose to study it further.

Brazilian jazz styles are as interesting rhythmically as they are harmonically. Fingerstyle bossa guitar has a rhythmic feel all its own. When the guitar covers bass and chords (and sometimes the melody), it can be quite complex. Chord progressions are equally unique and sometimes very unusual—even for jazz—so the best approach is to learn the rhythm first, then start moving the chords around. A typical rhythmic pattern, with the thumb playing steady bass notes against a syncopated upper chord, is broken down here.

Start with just the upper voicing of an Am7 chord. Pluck all three strings with your index, middle, and ring fingers. When the rhythm is comfortable, add bass notes on 1 and 3. All string damping is done with your picking hand; leave the chord in place, and play the bass notes "straight" with your thumb while your fingers damp the strings between every pluck of the chord.

When we add a second chord in measure 5, it *anticipates* the bass note in the next measure. This will almost always be true when the chords change in the middle of the two-bar pattern.

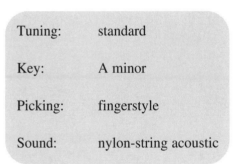

Tuning:	standard
Key:	A minor
Picking:	fingerstyle
Sound:	nylon-string acoustic

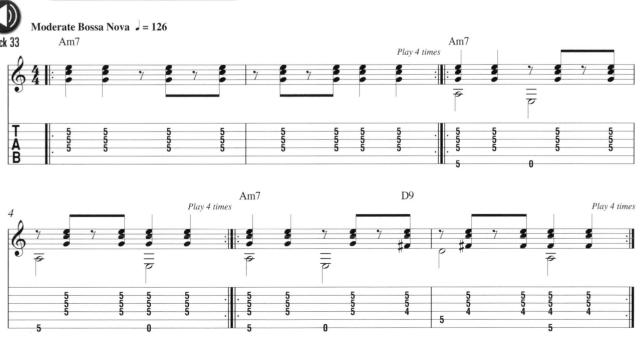

Moderate Bossa Nova ♩ = 126
Track 33

Now we can apply the rhythms to a chord progression, and add a few rhythmic changes as well. Nothing is this static in the real world of bossa nova; rhythms and chord variations can change at the players' discretion, as long as the composition is adhered to.

Tuning:	standard
Key:	D♭
Picking:	fingerstyle
Sound:	nylon-string acoustic

BOSSA 1

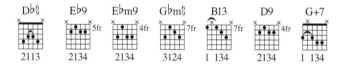

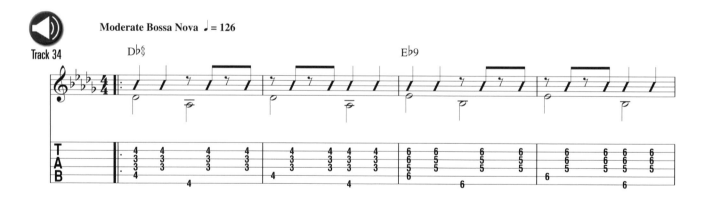

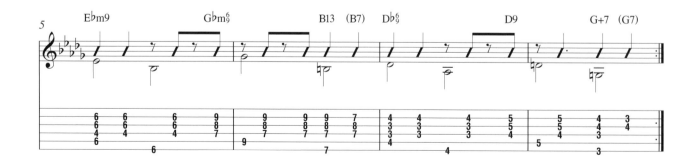

Again, all damping is done with the right hand. Hold left-hand positions until the changes, so that fretted bass notes keep sustaining after the chords are damped. Luckily, the right-hand picking pattern stays the same throughout, without having to jump or shift to different strings. That makes it easier to concentrate on the chord changes, which might not be a walk in the park for those of us who weren't weaned on jazz. Once you get them down, move on to the next example.

Now try varying the rhythm, so that the bass note anticipates the changes. The following variation has a more legato feel, with less chord muting, to match the forward rhythmic movement of the bass notes. When a bass note falls before the chord, it hits on the *upbeat*—"2-*and*" or "4-*and*"—along with the bass drum. Now the bass note takes the place of the chord that would have been played on "4-*and*," and the chord sustains through the change.

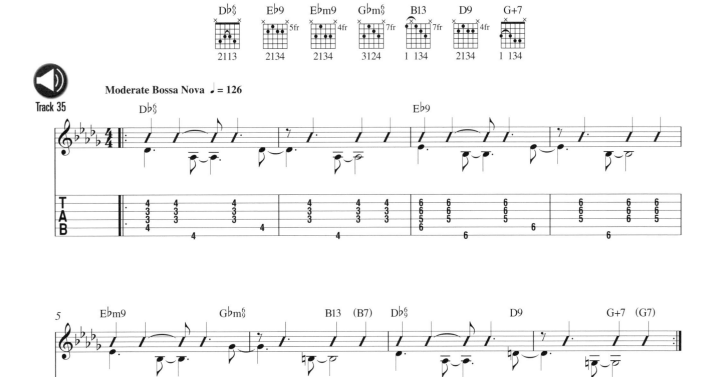

Brazilian jazz is a harmonic and rhythmic feast for the guitarist. For anyone who wants to play it professionally, it wouldn't hurt to know jazz theory inside and out—learn chords, positions, and alterations, so you can navigate the adventurous progressions of samba and bossa nova—and also to study Latin rhythms and practice the kind of fingerstyle techniques you see previewed here.

MEXICAN MARIACHI

Mexican vihuela (left) and guitarrón photos courtesy of Los Cenzontles Mexican Arts Center

Mariachi, like most Latin-American music, is *mestizo*—of mixed lineage, with roots in precolonial, Spanish, and African traditions—but the dynamic sounds of mariachi are pure Mexican. Modern mariachi groups can include chorus vocals, trumpets, violins, guitars, the *guitarrón* (a big guitar with a rich bass sound), and the vihuela—not the original Spanish vihuela, but a high-pitched variation of it, closely related to the Andean charango. The guitar, guitarrón, and vihuela play off of each other to create complex, syncopated rhythms, sometimes similar in sound and structure to Andean music, but with brighter-sounding chord progressions and more playful rhythmic interplay.

Early mariachi developed in Jalisco on the Pacific coast, based around a style known as *son*. As it gained popularity and spread throughout the country, many regional mariachi styles were created: rapid tempo *sones* (quick songs) and *románticas* (songs about romance), dance songs inspired by European forms, such as waltzes and polkas, and more locally relevant music like *guerrero*, dances of the farmers and cowboys. The following traditional tune, a showcase for the guitarrón/vihuela/guitar relationship, falls into the categories of the guerrero and sones. Listen for the hesitating feel of the guitarrón, contrasted with the driving strum of the vihuela.

Assuming you don't have a vihuela and guitarrón close by, those parts have been arranged for nylon-string guitar, while the third part for standard guitar is played on a steel-string. To accommodate the lower range of the guitarrón, Guitar 2 is in drop D tuning. Other guitars are in standard tuning. On the CD you can hear the low string for Guitar 2.

 Low D String

Track 36

Tuning:	Guitars 1 and 3, standard; Guitar 2, drop D
Key:	G
Picking:	Guitars 1 and 3, plectrum; Guitar 2, fingerstyle
Sound:	Guitars 1 and 2, nylon-string acoustic; Guitar 3, steel-string acoustic

TRIO MARIACHI

"Trio Mariachi" Performance Notes

If you're not very familiar with this style, you may be wondering why the guitarrón part sounds a little bit "off." This is the slightly behind-the-beat, neo-triplet feel that characterizes guitarrón playing in mariachi. The instrument serves to pull the other, busier parts back, and a slight push-and-pull between players is part of the mariachi sound. In effect, the bass part creates a kind of sub-rhythm.

Similar in arrangement to the Andean example, the opening vihuela part is played between frets 12 and 14 on Guitar 1. Between strums you add rhythmic slaps on the muted strings. It's best to start the intro with an upstroke on this part, so that your right hand instinctively keeps alternate strumming, even during rests. Then you're off and running with the melody, a combo of arpeggios and scale runs outlining a G chord in seventh position, while the steel-string plays rhythm in straight eighths. Framed by this very standard chord pattern, the three guitars play a dance with each other, stopping together at certain points, and bouncing rhythmically off each other at others. Pauses are important. Notice how the bass walks in threes after the breaks (meas. 15), a transitional signal that closes the B section.

When Guitar 3 takes the melody in section C, it is surrounded by an ordered chaos between the vihuela, which now double-mutes each strummed chord, and the off-beat bass. It's best to start the lead with the index finger on fret 10 so you can slide it down for the rest of the melody, then shift up back up to the tenth position as noted at measure 21. Then you're into some serious flatpicking in measure 24. Some of us find it best to alternate pick this throughout, but you might try playing the first three arpeggiated notes (A–C♯–E) as all downstrokes *(sweep picking)*. In any case, this is a challenging bit of melodic picking in pure mariachi style, outlining the chords as it goes. (The guitar melody of the mariachi classic "La Bamba" has a similar thing going on.)

The vihuela takes the melodic work again at measure 29, a sort of climactic turnaround that brings us back to the intro section with more rhythmic stops and syncopation.

If this seems like a busy tune, consider that the traditional version had more guitars, plus a female chorus singing three-part harmony vocals over the B section. A full mariachi band might play the piece with violins and/or trumpets, adding even more mass—and more sombreros—to the festive mariachi sound.

HAWAI'I: SLACK-KEY GUITAR

Ki ho'alu ("loosen the key"), the acoustic guitar playing style that came into worldwide prominence only recently, dates back to the early 1800s, when guitars were brought to the islands by Spanish and Mexican cowboys for hire. The instrument was soon adapted by their Hawaiian workmates, who incorporated what they had learned of Latino music into their traditional chants and songs to create a new, uniquely Hawaiian form of guitar music. They developed ways to get a full sound on one guitar by picking bass and chords with the thumb, while fingerpicking the melody or improvising on the higher-pitched strings. To accommodate this, the strings are tuned down to many different "slack" tunings, most of which contain a major chord and often a major 7th or 6th note.

At first, slack-key guitar playing accompanied vocal songs, but in the last century it has developed into a remarkable solo guitar tradition with techniques that mimic the yodels and falsettos of Hawaiian singing: lots of hammering on and pulling off, slides of single and multiple notes, and dynamic harmonics. The melody lines, often played in parallel 6ths, add to the warm, laid-back feel of the music that evokes waves and gentle tropical breezes.

Out of all the slack-key tunings (which are constantly being invented), a couple of the most popular are *taro patch* tuning (low to high, D–G–D–G–B–D) and F *wahine* tuning: (low to high, C–F–C–G–C–E). Our example will be in F wahine, a very open-sounding major tuning. "I Ka Po Me Ke Ao" ("Night and Day") is a popular slack-key standard. Originally a romantic vocal tune, it is arranged with a guitar melody in parallel 6ths, and the essential ki ho'alu techniques: slides, harmonics used within melodic phrases, hammer-and-pull slurs, and a bouncing "cowboy" bass line in 5ths (the first ten measures are a primer in this). Notice how the melody is stated once, ending on an upward inflection as a question, then repeated in an answer variation and punctuated with an affirming turnaround. Slack-key guitarists freely embellish their melodies, so no two performances of the same tune are likely to be the same.

Track 39

Tuning:	F wahine: (low to high) C–F–C–G–C–E
Scale/Key:	F major
Picking:	fingerstyle
Sound:	acoustic steel-string guitar (with lower strings heavy enough to tune down; light or mixed set)

I KA PO ME KE AO

Traditional

Track 40

F wahine tuning:
(low to high) C-F-C-G-C-E

Intro
Relaxed ♩ = 105

Track 41
slow demo
meas.
17–20,
27–28,
31–37 (on
repeat),
44–45

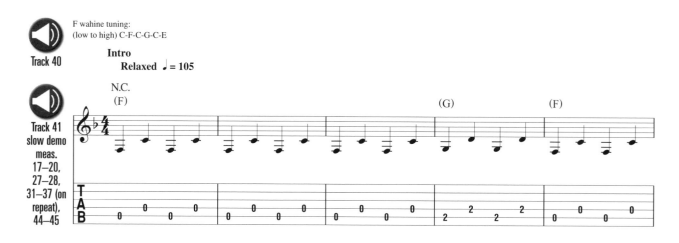

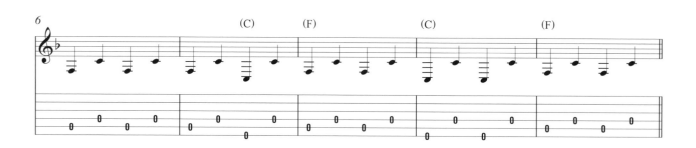

Verse

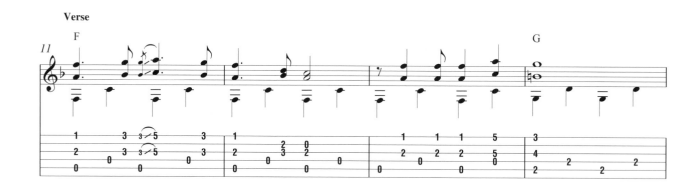

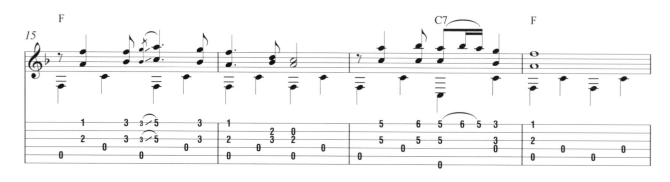

"I Ka Po Me Ke Ao" Performance Notes

Don't let the running length of this piece intimidate you. It's largely a series of variations on one theme, becoming subtly more complex as the tune progresses.

You might be familiar with the country and western Travis-picking technique, in which the thumb plays a bouncing bass line in 5ths while the fingers pluck a higher melody; traditional slack-key guitar relies on the same basic principle (reflecting its cowboy roots). This arrangement gives your thumb a head start. Once you're able to bounce the bass on autopilot, adding the double-note melody in the verse (meas. 11) should be relatively easy. Embellishing is the next step: slides, rhythmic variations, trills, etc. are coordinated with the bass line, so that the most awkward moves happen during the spaces (e.g., the trill in meas. 17).

The second verse (meas. 21) adds an open second string between the moving 6ths. Play the harmonic/hammer-on lick in measure 27 with the same laid-back feel as the rest of the tune—no rushing or extreme dynamics.

Keep it smooth and relaxed as the interlude gets into some busier fingerpicking and a first-finger barre on the B♭ chord in measure 32, followed by more "embedded" harmonics and, after the repeat, a frilly turnaround in measure 36. This utilizes another country-esque technique in which the thumb and fingers trade on adjacent strings with a hammer-on in between (suggested right-hand fingering is noted). Do not play this hard and heavy like a neurotic rock star! It can't be overstated that slack key is all about *aloha*—peaceful, calm good tidings. Every frill is balanced out by extra breathing space, as in measure 44, when the bass rests to give room to the upper trill. Finally, the ending is a nod to the Hawaiian *steel* guitar tradition: a major sixth chord (the ultimate resolving chord) sliding up an octave. Aloha, indeed!

SOURCE RECORDINGS AND RECOMMENDED MEDIA

AFRICA

Various Artists, *Africa: Colors of the World.* (CD) Allegro COTW 4
Afropop Worldwide. (PRI radio program) www.afropop.org
Native African Guitar. (DVD) Vestapol 13017

MIDDLE EAST

Various Artists, *Folklore of Turkey with "Saz."* (Cassette) Coskun Plak 83
Faramarz Payvar and Ensemble, *Iran: Persian Classical Music.* (CD) Elektra Nonesuch 9 72060-2
Hamza el Din, *The Water Wheel.* (CD) Nonesuch 72041-2

INDIA

Mynta, *Hot Madras.* (CD) Miramar 23072
Bonnie Wade, *Music in India: The Classical Traditions.* (Book) Manohar ISBN 81-85054-25-8
M. Nageswara Rao, *The Ten Graces Played on the Veena.* (LP) Nonesuch H-72027

CHINA

Lui Pui-yuen, *China: Music of the Pipa.* (CD) Elektra Nonesuch 9 72085-2
www.chinesepipa.com (Web site of pipa soloist Gao Hong)
Speaking in Tongues, *First Word.* (CD) Fathandz Music 002

JAPAN

Zumi-Kai Original Instrumental Group, *Koto Music of Japan.* (CD) LaserLight 12 184

SPAIN

Julian Bream, *Baroque Guitar.* (CD) RCA 60494
¡Guitarra! A Musical Journey through Spain. (DVD) Kultur D0067

IRELAND

Lehto and Wright, *Ye Mariners All.* (CD) New Folk/The Orchard B00005OLFR
Various Artists, *Past Masters of Irish Fiddle Music.* (CD) Topic 5O4VP

LATIN AMERICA

Andes: Various Artists, *Argentine Dances, Vol. 1.* (CD) Smithsonian Folkways 8841
Various Artists, *Flute, Guitar, and Harp of the Andes.* (CD) Legacy 321
www.rumillajta.com (Web site of Andean instrument specialist Manuel Navarro)

Brazil: Luiz Bonfá, *Guitar of Brazil.* (LP) Cook 1134
Antonio Carlos Jobim, *Wave.* (CD) A&M 812

Mexico: Mariachi Sol, *Mexico Lindo.* (CD) Arc EUCD 1249
Various Artists, *The Roots of the NarcoCorrido.* (CD) Arhoolie 7053
www.loscenzontles.com (Los Cenzontles Mexican Arts Center, San Francisco)

HAWAI'I

Ozzie Kotani, *Kani Ki Ho' Alu.* (CD) Windham Hill 38013
Keola Beamer, *Soliloquy.* (CD) Windham Hill B00005UK0Q

GUITAR NOTATION LEGEND

Guitar music can be notated three different ways: on a *musical staff*, in *tablature*, and in *rhythm slashes*.

RHYTHM SLASHES are written above the staff. Strum chords in the rhythm indicated. Use the chord diagrams found at the top of the first page of the transcription for the appropriate chord voicings. Round noteheads indicate single notes.

THE MUSICAL STAFF shows pitches and rhythms and is divided by bar lines into measures. Pitches are named after the first seven letters of the alphabet.

TABLATURE graphically represents the guitar fingerboard. Each horizontal line represents a a string, and each number represents a fret.

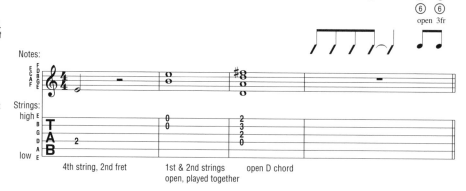

4th string, 2nd fret   1st & 2nd strings open, played together   open D chord

Definitions for Special Guitar Notation

HALF-STEP BEND: Strike the note and bend up 1/2 step.

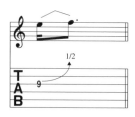

WHOLE-STEP BEND: Strike the note and bend up one step.

GRACE NOTE BEND: Strike the note and immediately bend up as indicated.

SLIGHT (MICROTONE) BEND: Strike the note and bend up 1/4 step.

BEND AND RELEASE: Strike the note and bend up as indicated, then release back to the original note. Only the first note is struck.

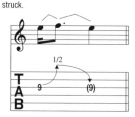

PRE-BEND: Bend the note as indicated, then strike it.

PRE-BEND AND RELEASE: Bend the note as indicated. Strike it and release the bend back to the original note.

UNISON BEND: Strike the two notes simultaneously and bend the lower note up to the pitch of the higher.

VIBRATO: The string is vibrated by rapidly bending and releasing the note with the fretting hand.

WIDE VIBRATO: The pitch is varied to a greater degree by vibrating with the fretting hand.

HAMMER-ON: Strike the first (lower) note with one finger, then sound the higher note (on the same string) with another finger by fretting it without picking.

PULL-OFF: Place both fingers on the notes to be sounded. Strike the first note and without picking, pull the finger off to sound the second (lower) note.

LEGATO SLIDE: Strike the first note and then slide the same fret-hand finger up or down to the second note. The second note is not struck.

SHIFT SLIDE: Same as legato slide, except the second note is struck.

TRILL: Very rapidly alternate between the notes indicated by continuously hammering on and pulling off.

TAPPING: Hammer ("tap") the fret indicated with the pick-hand index or middle finger and pull off to the note fretted by the fret hand.

70

NATURAL HARMONIC: Strike the note while the fret-hand lightly touches the string directly over the fret indicated.

Harm.

T
A 12
B

PINCH HARMONIC: The note is fretted normally and a harmonic is produced by adding the edge of the thumb or the tip of the index finger of the pick hand to the normal pick attack.

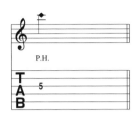

P.H.

T
A 5
B

HARP HARMONIC: The note is fretted normally and a harmonic is produced by gently resting the pick hand's index finger directly above the indicated fret (in parentheses) while the pick hand's thumb or pick assists by plucking the appropriate string.

8va

H.H.

T
A 7(19)
B

PICK SCRAPE: The edge of the pick is rubbed down (or up) the string, producing a scratchy sound.

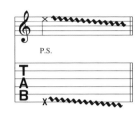

P.S.

T
A
B X

MUFFLED STRINGS: A percussive sound is produced by laying the fret hand across the string(s) without depressing, and striking them with the pick hand.

T
A x
B x

PALM MUTING: The note is partially muted by the pick hand lightly touching the string(s) just before the bridge.

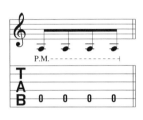

P.M. - - - - - - - - - - - - -

T
A
B 0   0   0   0

RAKE: Drag the pick across the strings indicated with a single motion.

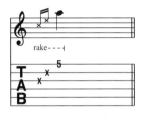

rake - - - -|

T
A 5
B x

TREMOLO PICKING: The note is picked as rapidly and continuously as possible.

T
A 5   7
B

ARPEGGIATE: Play the notes of the chord indicated by quickly rolling them from bottom to top.

T   5
A   5
B   5
    5

VIBRATO BAR DIVE AND RETURN: The pitch of the note or chord is dropped a specified number of steps (in rhythm) then returned to the original pitch.

w/ bar

T
A 0   (0)
B

-1

VIBRATO BAR SCOOP: Depress the bar just before striking the note, then quickly release the bar.

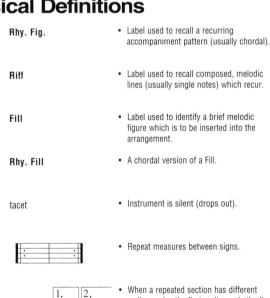

w/ bar - - - - - - - - -|

T
A ⌐4 ⌐5 ⌐7
B

VIBRATO BAR DIP: Strike the note and then immediately drop a specified number of steps, then release back to the original pitch.

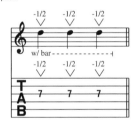

-1/2   -1/2   -1/2
 V   V   V

w/ bar - - - - - - - - - - - -|

-1/2   -1/2   -1/2
 V   V   V

T
A 7   7   7
B

Additional Musical Definitions

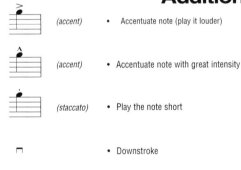

(accent)	• Accentuate note (play it louder)
(accent)	• Accentuate note with great intensity
(staccato)	• Play the note short
⌐	• Downstroke
V	• Upstroke
D.S. al Coda	• Go back to the sign (𝄋), then play until the measure marked "**To Coda**," then skip to the section labelled "**Coda**."
D.C. al Fine	• Go back to the beginning of the song and play until the measure marked "**Fine**" (end).

Rhy. Fig.	• Label used to recall a recurring accompaniment pattern (usually chordal).
Riff	• Label used to recall composed, melodic lines (usually single notes) which recur.
Fill	• Label used to identify a brief melodic figure which is to be inserted into the arrangement.
Rhy. Fill	• A chordal version of a Fill.
tacet	• Instrument is silent (drops out).
	• Repeat measures between signs.
1. 2.	• When a repeated section has different endings, play the first ending only the first time and the second ending only the second time.

NOTE: Tablature numbers in parentheses mean:
1. The note is being sustained over a system (note in standard notation is tied), or
2. The note is sustained, but a new articulation (such as a hammer-on, pull-off, slide or vibrato begins), or
3. The note is a barely audible "ghost" note (note in standard notation is also in parentheses).

ABOUT THE AUTHOR

Musician, composer, writer, and visual artist Greg P. Herriges resides in Minneapolis, Minnesota, performs and records with cross-cultural ensembles and as a solo acoustic artist, teaches guitar, and writes/edits/produces music instruction books and DVDs for Hal Leonard Corporation. He has fronted original avant-rock groups, played lead guitar with various pop and fusion acts, and studied ethnomusicology with an emphasis on Asian art music. His latest music is available on New Folk Records (www.newfolkrecords.com), and more musical journeys are at www.gregherriges.com.